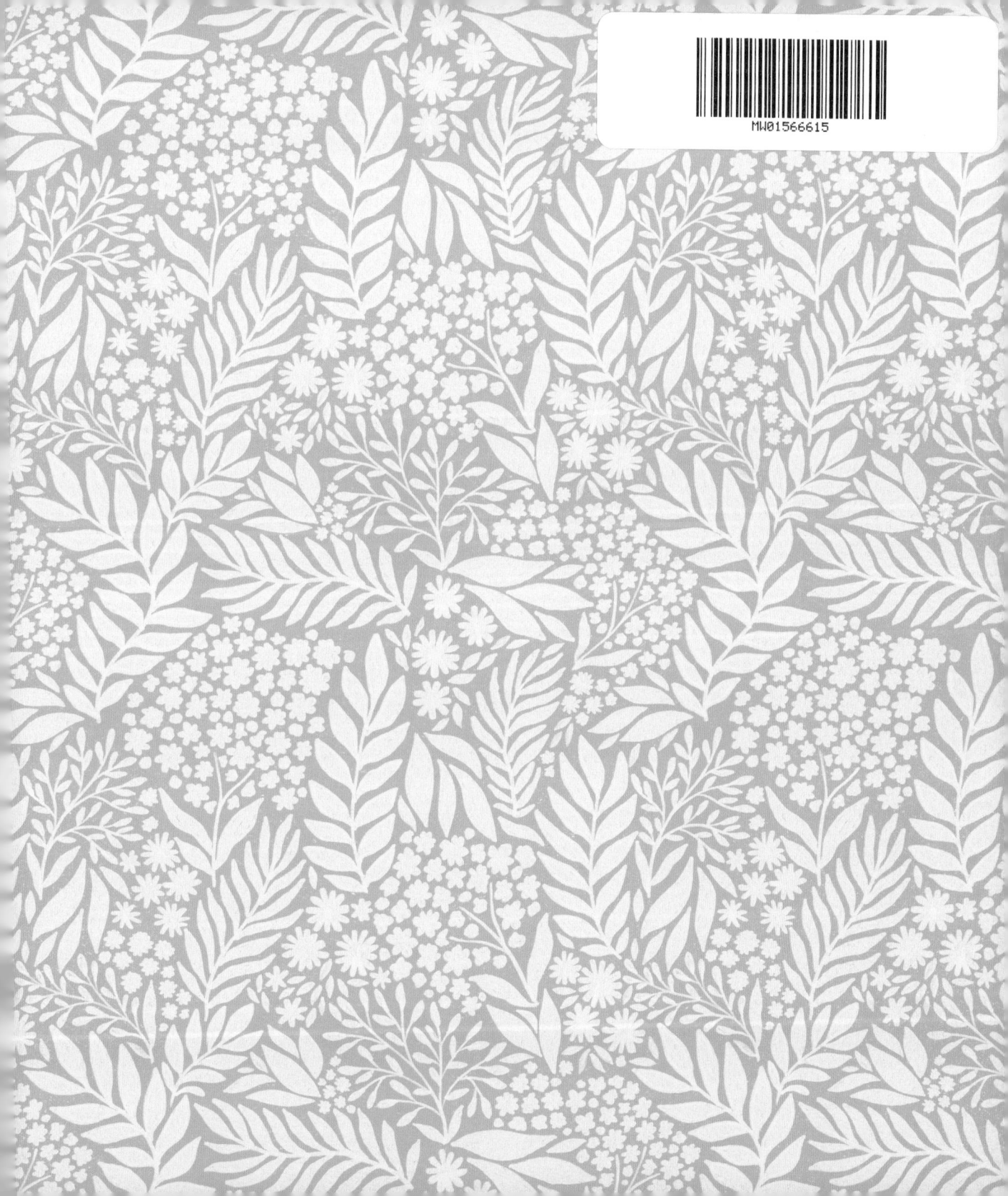

The Story of Us

This is the story of us.

It's the story of what is, and the story of what will be. It's something we could only write together—the story of our loving and living.

Like all stories, its beauty is in its complexity. There are days when laughter carries us... there are moments we'll cherish forever... there are times when the challenges shape everything.

This is our place to capture it all—a space for this story we share. Because all of it is ours... and all of it is worth remembering.

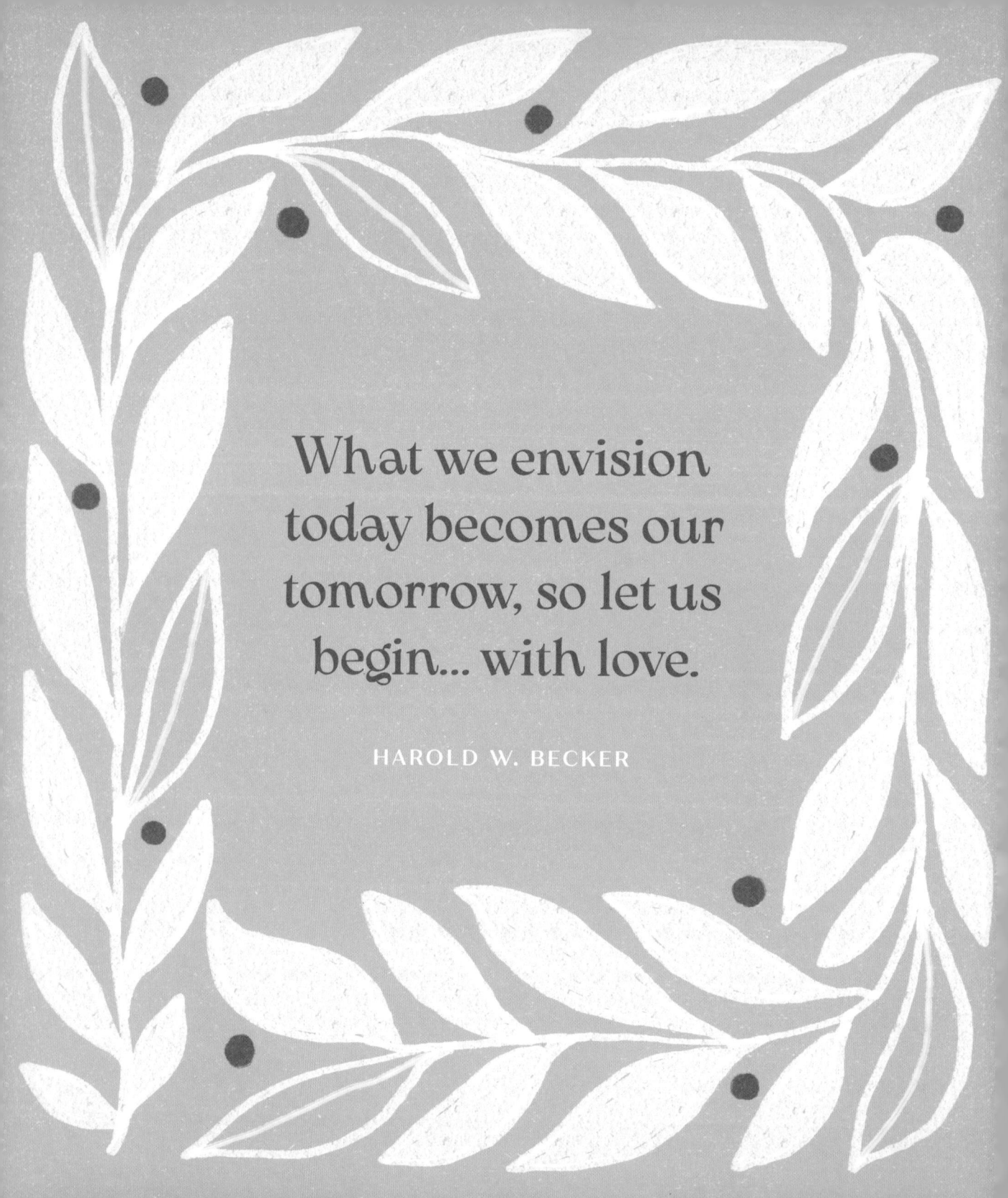

What we envision today becomes our tomorrow, so let us begin... with love.

HAROLD W. BECKER

YEAR:

THIS IS OUR _____ ANNIVERSARY:

A moment from this year I (_____) always want to remember:
                                    name

_____

_____

_____

_____

A moment from this year I (_____) always want to remember:
                                    name

_____

_____

_____

_____

Shared reflections

These are some things we love about us:

_____
_____
_____
_____

Something we want to try to always make time for:

_____
_____
_____
_____

Some things we're really looking forward to:

_____
_____
_____
_____

An intention we have for the coming year:

Milestones

This was the year we:

YEAR:

THIS IS OUR _____
ANNIVERSARY:

A moment from this year I (_____) always want to remember:
                            name

_____
_____
_____
_____
_____

A moment from this year I (_____) always want to remember:
                            name

_____
_____
_____
_____
_____

Shared reflections

A few of our favorite rituals or routines:

_____
_____
_____
_____
_____

These are some ways we have changed for the better this year:

_____
_____
_____
_____
_____

Let's give ourselves credit for:

_____
_____
_____
_____
_____

Looking to the future, we want to make sure we continue:

_____
_____
_____
_____
_____
_____

Milestones

This was the year we:

_____
_____
_____
_____
_____

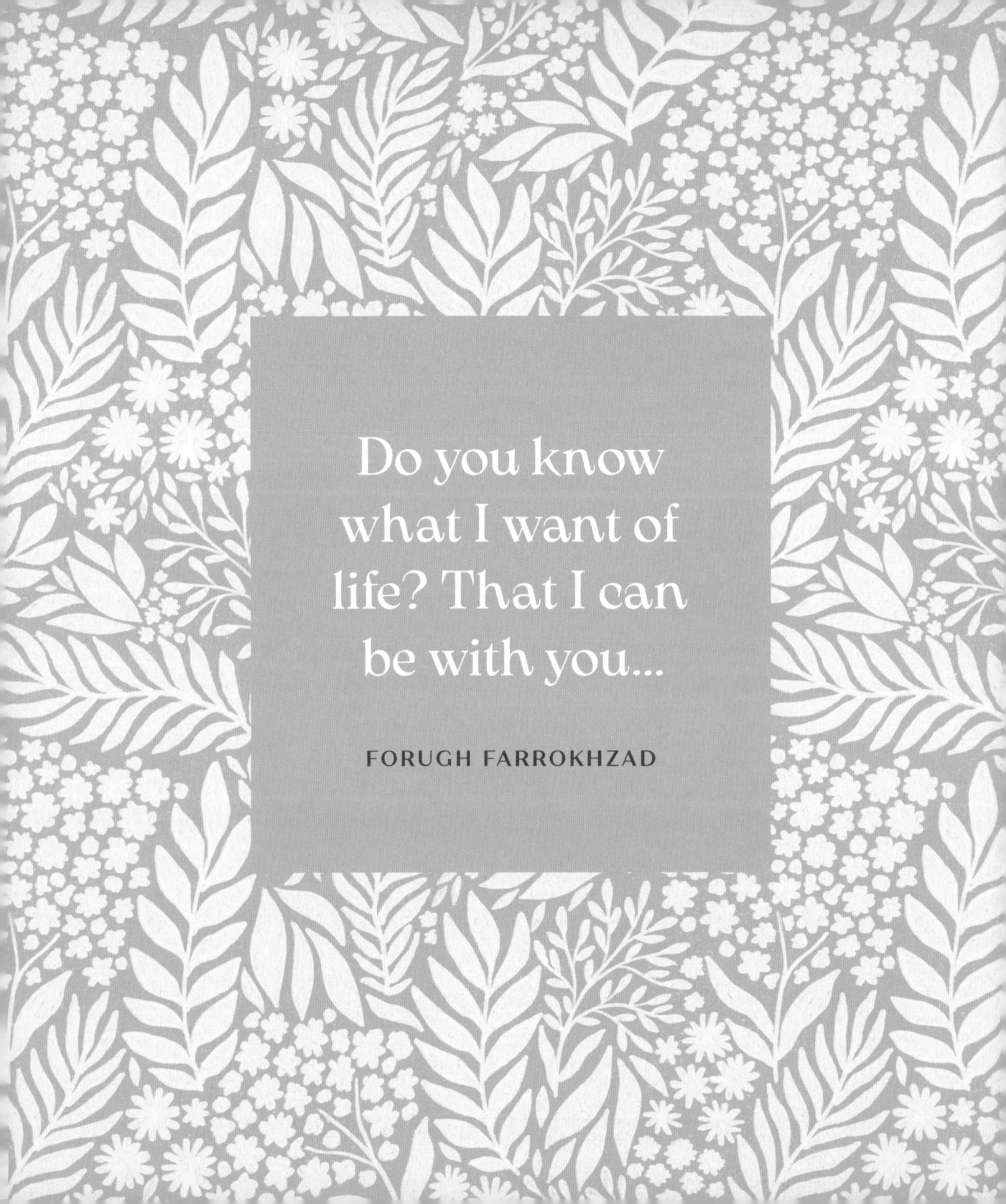

Do you know what I want of life? That I can be with you...

FORUGH FARROKHZAD

YEAR:

THIS IS OUR _____ ANNIVERSARY:

A moment from this year I (_____) always want to remember:
　　　　　　　　　　　　　　　　　　　　name

_____
_____
_____
_____
_____

A moment from this year I (_____) always want to remember:
　　　　　　　　　　　　　　　　　　　　name

_____
_____
_____
_____
_____

Shared reflections

This year, we discovered:

_____
_____
_____
_____
_____

Some of our greatest strengths as a couple:

_____
_____
_____
_____
_____

A challenge we met and overcame:

_____
_____
_____
_____
_____

Something we want to keep improving on:

_____
_____
_____
_____
_____

Milestones

This was the year we:

_____
_____
_____
_____
_____

We can only learn
to love by loving.

IRIS MURDOCH

YEAR:

THIS IS OUR ____
ANNIVERSARY:

A moment from this year I (_____) always want to remember:
                              name

_____
_____
_____
_____
_____

A moment from this year I (_____) always want to remember:
                              name

_____
_____
_____
_____
_____

Shared reflections

Something we're really proud of ourselves for:

_____
_____
_____
_____
_____

Some of the most meaningful ways we spend time together:

_____
_____
_____
_____
_____

A little moment that showed us something big about ourselves:

_____
_____
_____
_____
_____

A tradition we want to begin (or continue):

_____
_____
_____
_____
_____
_____

Milestones

This was the year we:

_____
_____
_____
_____
_____
_____

We honor everything we have been.
We cherish everything we are.
We look forward to all we are yet to be.

We are still in the process of writing
our complex and beautiful story.

Our goal should be
to achieve joy.

ANA CASTILLO

YEAR:

THIS IS OUR _____ ANNIVERSARY:

A moment from this year I (_____) always want to remember:
name

_____
_____
_____
_____
_____

A moment from this year I (_____) always want to remember:
name

_____
_____
_____
_____
_____

Shared reflections

Five years ago, I don't think we could possibly have imagined:

_____
_____
_____
_____
_____

A collection of our greatest joyful moments together:

_____
_____
_____
_____
_____

In the difficult moments, we want to always try to:

_____
_____
_____
_____
_____

For the next five years, we want to focus on:

_____
_____
_____
_____
_____
_____

Milestones

This was the year we:

_____
_____
_____
_____
_____
_____

Decide first what is authentic, then go after it with all your heart.

LOUISE ERDRICH

YEAR:

THIS IS OUR _____ ANNIVERSARY:

A moment from this year I (_____) always want to remember:
　　　　　　　　　　　　　　　　　　　name

_____
_____
_____
_____
_____

A moment from this year I (_____) always want to remember:
　　　　　　　　　　　　　　　　　　　name

_____
_____
_____
_____
_____

Shared reflections

These are some quirks we love about our partnership:

_____
_____
_____
_____

Something we're outgrowing is:

_____
_____
_____
_____

Something we're growing toward is:

_____
_____
_____
_____

A gift (tangible or intangible) we want to give ourselves this year:

_____
_____
_____
_____
_____

Milestones

This was the year we:

_____
_____
_____
_____

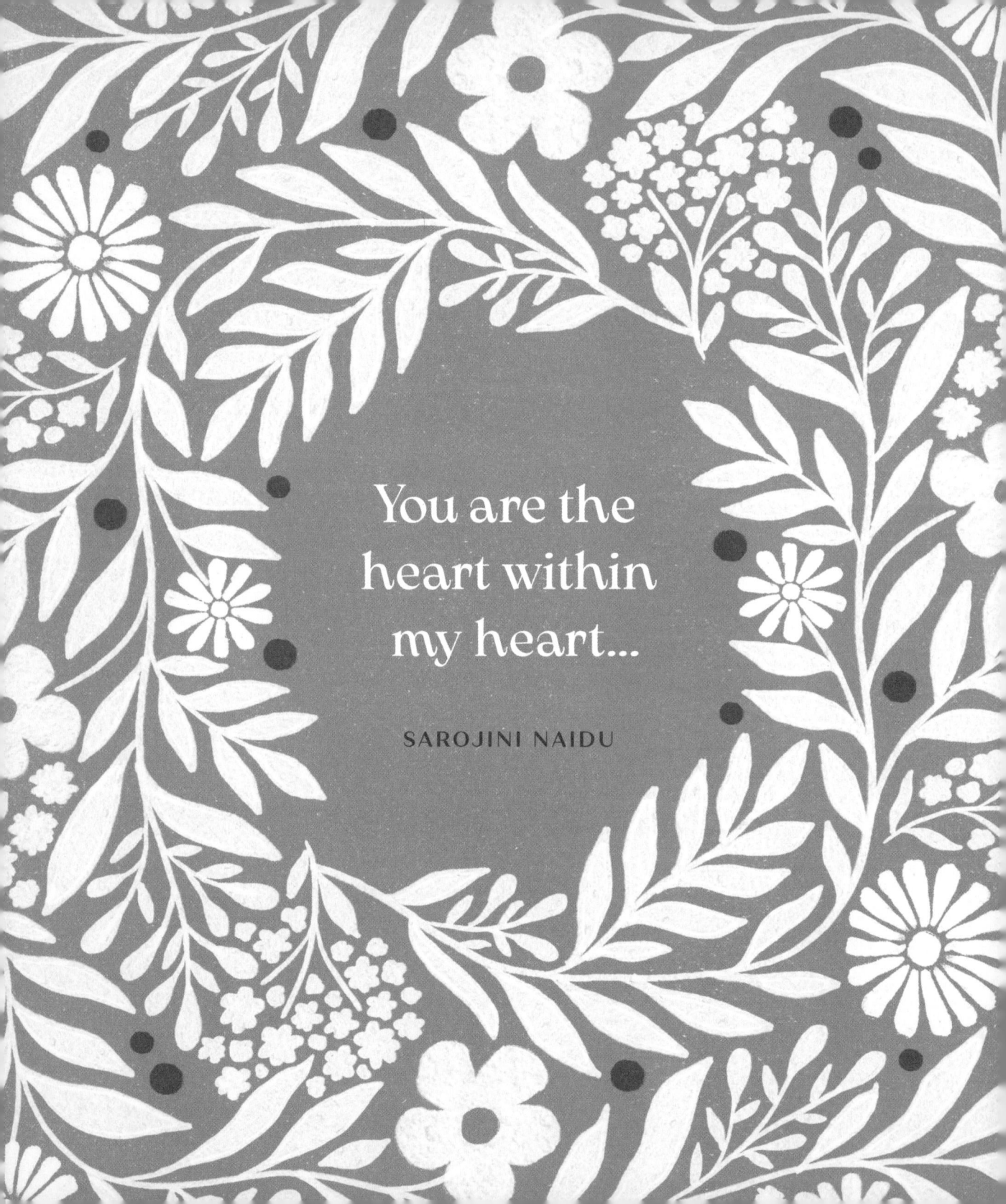

YEAR:

THIS IS OUR _____ ANNIVERSARY:

A moment from this year I (_____) always want to remember:
_{name}

_____
_____
_____
_____
_____

A moment from this year I (_____) always want to remember:
_{name}

_____
_____
_____
_____
_____

Shared reflections

Something we do remarkably well together:

_____
_____
_____
_____
_____

A secret fact about us that not many people know:

_____
_____
_____
_____
_____

Some little things that mean a lot to us:

_____
_____
_____
_____
_____

Something we used to do that we want to return to:

___
___
___
___
___
___

Milestones

This was the year we:

___
___
___
___
___

YEAR:

THIS IS OUR ____
ANNIVERSARY:

A moment from this year I (_____) always want to remember:
                              name

_____
_____
_____
_____
_____

A moment from this year I (_____) always want to remember:
                              name

_____
_____
_____
_____
_____

Shared reflections

Some things we will never get tired of:

_____
_____
_____
_____
_____

This always brings us together:

_____
_____
_____
_____
_____

If we were to give ourselves an award for anything this year, it would be:

_____
_____
_____
_____
_____

Something we want to commit to working on:

_____
_____
_____
_____
_____
_____

Milestones

This was the year we:

_____
_____
_____
_____
_____
_____

What a gift to have spent so much time together... to watch the days become years.

Today, we celebrate the work and the love that have brought us both here.

The choice to love is a choice to connect—to find ourselves in the other.

BELL HOOKS

YEAR:

THIS IS OUR _____ ANNIVERSARY:

A moment from this year I (_____) always want to remember:
                              name

_____
_____
_____
_____
_____

A moment from this year I (_____) always want to remember:
                              name

_____
_____
_____
_____
_____

Shared reflections

A difficult thing that has brought us closer:

_____

_____

_____

_____

A new thing we tried that we want to keep doing:

_____

_____

_____

_____

Something we've been making great progress on:

_____

_____

_____

_____

We're determined to make this coming year the year that we:

_____
_____
_____
_____
_____

Milestones

This was the year we:

_____
_____
_____
_____
_____

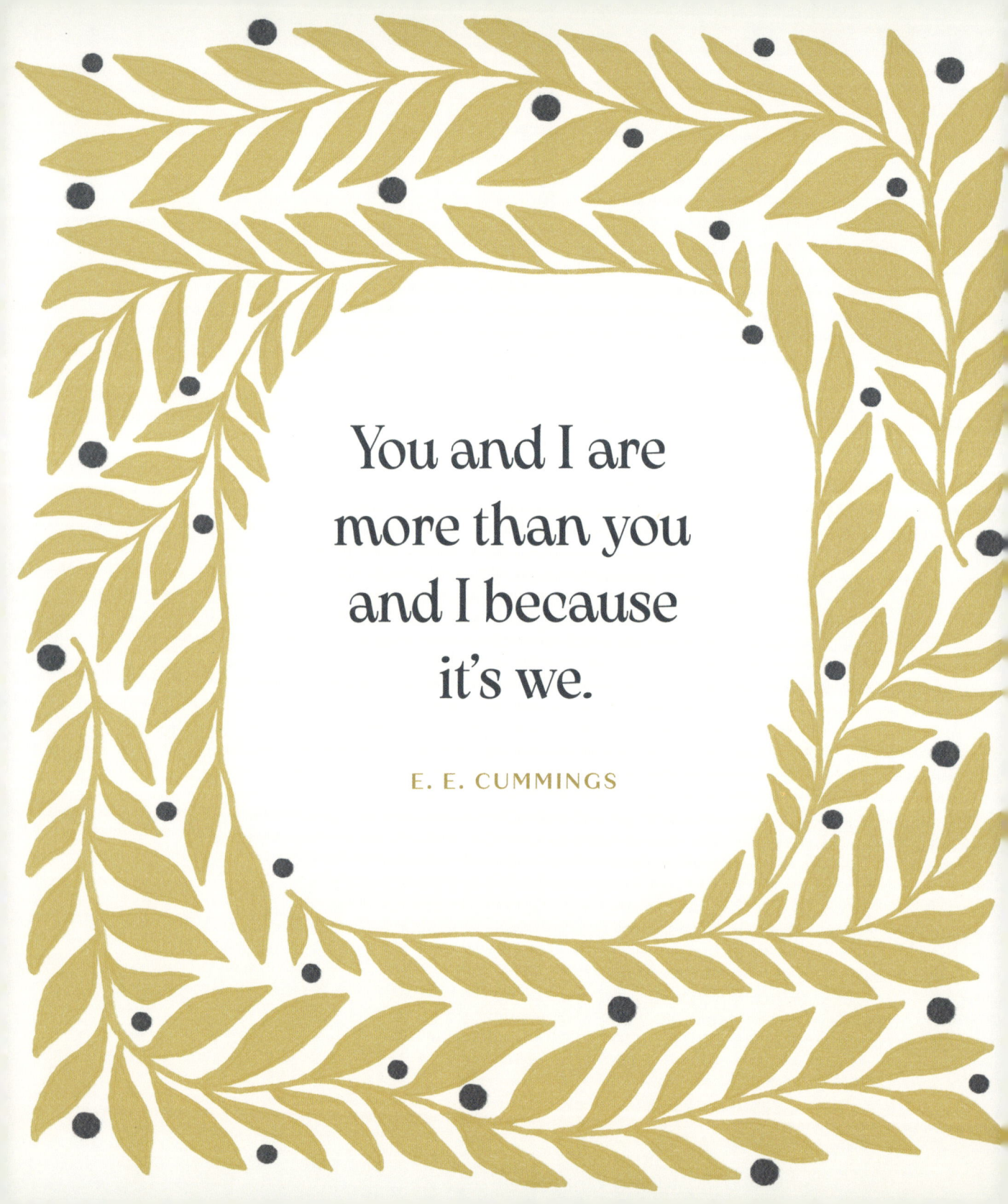

YEAR:

THIS IS OUR _____
ANNIVERSARY:

A moment from this year I (_____) always want to remember:
                              name

_____
_____
_____
_____
_____

A moment from this year I (_____) always want to remember:
                              name

_____
_____
_____
_____
_____

Shared reflections

Ten years ago, we could never have imagined:

_____
_____
_____
_____
_____

Some things we love about the couple we have become:

_____
_____
_____
_____
_____

Areas where our hard work has paid off:

_____
_____
_____
_____
_____

A big dream or goal for our next ten years:

_____
_____
_____
_____
_____

Milestones

This was the year we:

_____
_____
_____
_____
_____

YEAR:

THIS IS OUR _____
ANNIVERSARY:

A moment from this year I (_____) always want to remember:
                            name

_____
_____
_____
_____
_____

A moment from this year I (_____) always want to remember:
                            name

_____
_____
_____
_____
_____

Shared reflections

Something we're wonderfully silly about:

_____
_____
_____
_____
_____

Something we're wonderfully serious about:

_____
_____
_____
_____
_____

Some things we both love equally:

_____
_____
_____
_____
_____

A wish we want to make together:

_____
_____
_____
_____
_____
_____

Milestones

This was the year we:

_____
_____
_____
_____
_____
_____

Love is the whole thing.
We are only pieces.

RUMI

YEAR:

THIS IS OUR _____
ANNIVERSARY:

A moment from this year I (_____) always want to remember:
                                    name

_____
_____
_____
_____

A moment from this year I (_____) always want to remember:
                                    name

_____
_____
_____
_____

Shared reflections

One of the most unique things about us as a couple is the way we:

_____
_____
_____
_____
_____

These are some skills we've really refined over the years:

_____
_____
_____
_____
_____

These are a few of our favorite places, whether far away or nearby:

_____
_____
_____
_____
_____

Something we look forward to continuing:

_____
_____
_____
_____
_____
_____

Milestones

This was the year we:

_____
_____
_____
_____
_____
_____

There is a story, a love,
a language that is ours and ours alone.

My life is forever tied to yours.
And my heart calls your heart home.

YEAR:

THIS IS OUR _____
ANNIVERSARY:

A moment from this year I (_____) always want to remember:
_{name}

_____
_____
_____
_____
_____

A moment from this year I (_____) always want to remember:
_{name}

_____
_____
_____
_____
_____

Shared reflections

Something truly remarkable about our relationship is:

_____
_____
_____
_____
_____

This year, we feel really fortunate to:

_____
_____
_____
_____
_____

A few wishes we once made that have come true for us:

_____
_____
_____
_____
_____

Some things we never want to take for granted:

_____
_____
_____
_____
_____

Milestones

This was the year we:

_____
_____
_____
_____
_____

Love... has to be made, like bread; re-made all the time, made new.

URSULA K. LE GUIN

YEAR:

THIS IS OUR _____ ANNIVERSARY:

A moment from this year I (_____) always want to remember:
name

_____
_____
_____
_____
_____

A moment from this year I (_____) always want to remember:
name

_____
_____
_____
_____
_____

Shared reflections

This is something that maybe no one outside of our relationship knows:

_____
_____
_____
_____

One of the healthiest things about our partnership is:

_____
_____
_____
_____

A challenging situation we really rose to meet:

_____
_____
_____
_____

A promise we want to make ourselves for the coming year:

Milestones

This was the year we:

It has made
me better,
loving you.

HENRY JAMES

YEAR:

THIS IS OUR _____
ANNIVERSARY:

A moment from this year I (_____) always want to remember:
                              name

_____
_____
_____
_____
_____

A moment from this year I (_____) always want to remember:
                              name

_____
_____
_____
_____
_____

Shared reflections

Lately, we've found a lot of joy and meaning in:

_____
_____
_____
_____
_____

A small thing we started doing that's made a big difference:

_____
_____
_____
_____
_____

This year, we're grateful for:

_____
_____
_____
_____
_____

Something we want to do this year to keep our relationship strong is:

_____
_____
_____
_____
_____

Milestones

This was the year we:

_____
_____
_____
_____
_____

Your heart and
my heart are very,
very old friends.

HĀFEZ

YEAR:

THIS IS OUR ____
ANNIVERSARY:

A moment from this year I (_____) always want to remember:
_{name}

_____

_____

_____

_____

A moment from this year I (_____) always want to remember:
_{name}

_____

_____

_____

_____

Shared reflections

These are some things we get better and better at:

_____
_____
_____
_____
_____

These are some of the unchanging things we love about our relationship:

_____
_____
_____
_____
_____

Our younger selves would probably be so surprised that we:

_____
_____
_____
_____
_____

In the coming year, we want to challenge ourselves to:

_____
_____
_____
_____
_____
_____

Milestones

This was the year we:

_____
_____
_____
_____
_____

Let us fully celebrate the years that we have shared... the joys and the challenges, the things that have stayed steady, the things that have changed.

No matter what the years will bring, may our love always remain.

...love is always new.

PAULO COELHO

YEAR:

THIS IS OUR _____ ANNIVERSARY:

A moment from this year I (_____) always want to remember:
_{name}

_____
_____
_____
_____
_____

A moment from this year I (_____) always want to remember:
_{name}

_____
_____
_____
_____
_____

Shared reflections

Some of our favorite new experiences this year were:

_____
_____
_____
_____
_____

A few ways we are still learning and growing:

_____
_____
_____
_____
_____

We want to applaud ourselves for:

_____
_____
_____
_____
_____

The next big thing or things on our horizon:
___
___
___
___
___
___

Milestones

This was the year we:
___
___
___
___
___

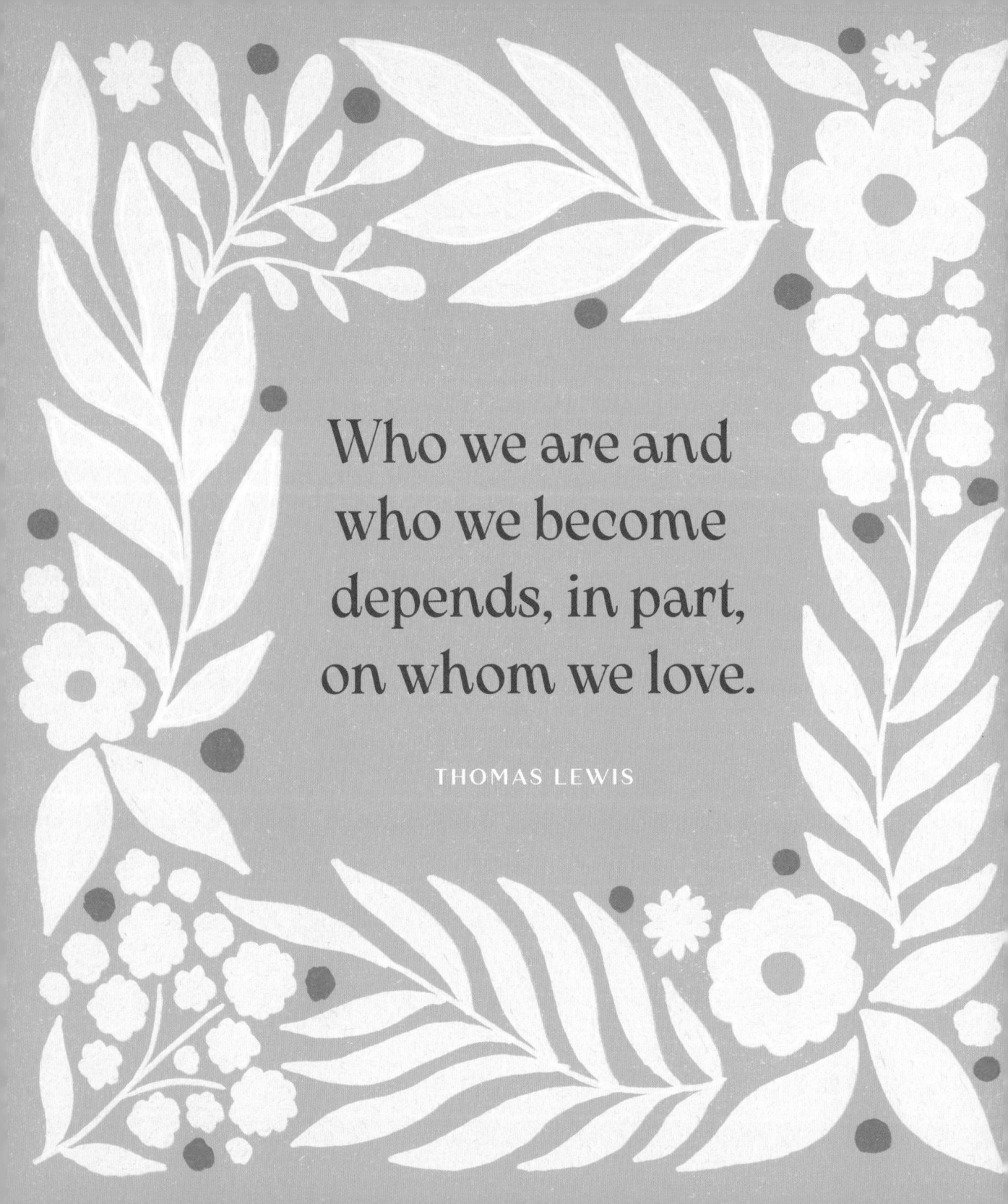

Who we are and who we become depends, in part, on whom we love.

THOMAS LEWIS

YEAR:

THIS IS OUR _____ ANNIVERSARY:

A moment from this year I (_____) always want to remember:
                              name

_____
_____
_____
_____
_____

A moment from this year I (_____) always want to remember:
                              name

_____
_____
_____
_____
_____

Shared reflections

Some new things we discovered this year:

_____
_____
_____
_____
_____

Some things we're so glad we've done this whole time:

_____
_____
_____
_____
_____

One of our secrets to a lasting relationship:

_____
_____
_____
_____
_____

Some good things we think (or know) this year will hold:

_____
_____
_____
_____
_____
_____

Milestones

This was the year we:

_____
_____
_____
_____
_____
_____

We are free to change.
And love changes us.

WALTER MOSLEY

YEAR:

THIS IS OUR _____
ANNIVERSARY:

A moment from this year I (_____) always want to remember:
                              name

_____
_____
_____
_____
_____

A moment from this year I (_____) always want to remember:
                              name

_____
_____
_____
_____
_____

Shared reflections

One of the biggest ways we've evolved together is:

_____
_____
_____
_____
_____

Some of our greatest shared accomplishments include:

_____
_____
_____
_____
_____

A skill we continue to strengthen together is:

_____
_____
_____
_____
_____

This year, we are committed to:

_____
_____
_____
_____
_____
_____

Milestones

This was the year we:

_____
_____
_____
_____
_____
_____

YEAR:

THIS IS OUR _____
ANNIVERSARY:

A moment from this year I (_____) always want to remember:
_{name}

_____
_____
_____
_____
_____

A moment from this year I (_____) always want to remember:
_{name}

_____
_____
_____
_____
_____

Shared reflections

Some of our favorite highlights of the last two decades include:

_____
_____
_____
_____
_____

Looking back over this book, we're surprised or delighted to see:

_____
_____
_____
_____
_____

Some of the things we respect most deeply about our partnership are:

_____
_____
_____
_____
_____

Something new we want to begin this year:

_____
_____
_____
_____
_____

Milestones

This was the year we:

_____
_____
_____
_____
_____

The story of us is long and
complex, beautiful and true.

It's a story we love...
a story we write together...
a story that continues.

Two Decades of People and Places

These are some people who have supported us through the years, and the ways they made a difference:

NAME: _____

They helped us by:

_____
_____

NAME: _____

They helped us by:

_____
_____

NAME: _____

They helped us by:

_____
_____

NAME: _____

They helped us by:

_____
_____

These are some places that have shaped our last two decades, and why they're so important:

PLACE: _____

What it means to us:

_____
_____

PLACE: _____

What it means to us:

_____
_____

PLACE: _____

What it means to us:

_____
_____

PLACE: _____

What it means to us:

_____
_____

Two Decades of Growth and Change

Looking back, these are some of the things the *EASY YEARS* gave us or taught us:

_____
_____
_____
_____
_____
_____

Looking back, these are some of the things the *DIFFICULT YEARS* gave us or taught us:

_____
_____
_____
_____
_____
_____

In these ways, we are deeply *SIMILAR* to the people we were two decades ago:

_____
_____
_____
_____
_____
_____
_____

In these ways, we are deeply *DIFFERENT* from the people we were two decades ago:

_____
_____
_____
_____
_____
_____
_____

A Letter to Each Other

A letter from me, _____ **, to you,** _____

Thank you so much for:

_____

_____

_____

I love the way we:

_____

_____

_____

These past years have taught me:

_____

_____

_____

I look forward to:

_____

_____

_____

A letter from me, _____ **, to you,** _____

Thank you so much for:

_____
_____
_____

I love the way we:

_____
_____
_____

These past years have taught me:

_____
_____
_____

I look forward to:

_____
_____
_____

Written and Compiled by: M.H. Clark
Designed by: Jessica Phoenix
Edited by: Bailey Vega

ISBN: 978-1-957891-12-5

© 2024 by Compendium, Inc. All rights reserved. No part of this publication may be reproduced or transmitted in any form or by any means, electronic or mechanical, including photocopy, recording, or any storage and retrieval system now known or to be invented without written permission from the publisher. Contact: Compendium, Inc., 1420 80th Street SW, Suite C, Everett, WA 98203. *The Story of Us: An Anniversary Keepsake Book of Years, Days, and Memories*; Compendium; live inspired; and the format, design, layout, and coloring used in this book are trademarks and/or trade dress of Compendium, Inc. This book may be ordered directly from the publisher, but please try your local bookstore first. Call us at 800.91.IDEAS, or come see our full line of inspiring products at live-inspired.com.

1st printing. Printed in China with soy inks on FSC®-Mix certified paper.

Create meaningful moments with gifts that inspire.

CONNECT WITH US
live-inspired.com | sayhello@compendiuminc.com

    @compendiumliveinspired
#compendiumliveinspired